# How to Build a Successful Hypnotherapy Business

## 50 tips and tricks

by Jennie Kitching

Copyright © Jennie Kitching and Brit Whittaker 2016

The rights of Jennie Kitching and Brit Whittaker to be identified as the authors of this work has been asserted by them in accordance with the Copyright, Designs and Patents Act, 1988. All rights reserved. Without limiting the rights under copyrights above, no part of this publication may be reproduced, stored in, or introduced into a retrieval system, or transmitted, in any form or by any means (electronic, mechanical, photocopying, recording, or otherwise), without the express prior written permission of the copyright owners aforementioned.

By purchasing this book you agree that you have read and understand that all information is subject to the reader's interpretation. The authors will not be held accountable for any interpretations or decisions made by recipients based on information provided herein.

This information is for education and entertainment purposes only. All information and/or advice given to you herein should not take the place of any medical, legal or financial advice given to you by any qualified professional. Any names or characters within this book are the product of the author's imagination and any resemblance to real persons, living or dead is completely coincidental.

DISCLAIMER: This book is written and published to provide readers with real life tips about how I have built success in my business. Traditionally a lonely profession, my intention in writing this work is to bring together the best advice from the best source, ie real life, to save you the trials and errors I have been through myself and to impart as much useful information as possible on what works in the real world. No one can guarantee that you will be a success as this is up to you, which means you have the power within you right now to do the best you possibly can to be the best you can possibly be. It is my genuine intent that you benefit enormously from the information herein which is offered in good faith. In order to benefit from the information in this book you must put the information into action. Merely reading a book cannot do anything for your business. The techniques will have variable levels of success depending upon where you live and practice hypnosis. Use the feedback you receive from putting these tips into practice and, if you find your location is a problem, then move location! It is up to you. You are more resourceful than you think. Environment is only one factor in all this, though it is a big one. Identify what needs to change and improve and do it. The only way to determine how this information can help you to be successful is to examine each tip and use your own good sense to apply it in your own circumstances and evaluate your results.

*Dedicated to all my followers, supporters and Hypnotherapists embarking on this great voyage into the remarkable powers of the human mind-* Jennie

# Author Biography

Jennie Kitching ADPR SQHP –

A teacher of The Advanced Diploma in Hypnosis and A Master Hypnotist since 2003, Jennie was awarded her first training qualification in 1994. Since that time she has become a certified trainer of a variety of differing methodologies in the corporate and private sector (including Louise Hay, '*You Can Heal Your Life*', Susan Jeffers ('*Feel the Fear and Do It Anyway*'). Additional study, notably of the works published by John Cleese and Robin Skynner ('*Life and How to Survive It)*' enabled Jennie to incorporate the more personal aspects of self-improvement into the traditional corporate training arena (GKN, Dudley MBC, The Law Society, etc) designing and delivering bespoke courses such as Pre-Retirement and Women's Development. Jennie presents with humour and enthusiasm drawing on this extensive knowledge base. Now she writes, teaches, continues her private consultations and delivers this knowledge to as many people as possible! You can contact her at info@hiprocom.com.

Jennie Kitching also has the accolade of being a GHR Accredited Advanced Senior Hypnotherapist, one of only a few in the world and now teaches others to that level.

She loves swimming underwater, plays the Ukulele and is an avid Cosplay enthusiast.

# Thank you for reading!

Amazon reviews are really important to future writing projects for independent authors. Please leave a review for me because I would love to hear your thoughts about this book.

If you would like to receive your **FREE** preview of my next book please **email** info@hiprocom.com.

Thank you!

..........................................

## CONTENTS

AUTHOR BIOGRAPHY ..................................................................4
MARKETING ...............................................................................9
HOW TO GET MORE CLIENTS ......................................................10
   *1 Take Action Now or Don't ..............................................10*
   *2 Beating Yourself Up .......................................................11*
   *3 If it works do it .............................................................11*
   *4 Free pays off..................................................................12*
   *5 The Clubs ......................................................................13*
   *6 Focused Workshops ......................................................14*
   *7 Back to School ..............................................................14*
   *8 Accelerated learning programs.....................................15*
   *9 Your car can make you a star........................................15*
   *10 Everywhere you go people ought to know..................16*
   *11 Loud and proud ...........................................................17*
   *12 Being a Groupie ..........................................................17*
   *13 Article Writing.............................................................18*
   *14 Cashing in on Coupons ................................................18*
   *15 Event Listings .............................................................19*
   *16 Taking the Pressure Off...............................................19*
MONEY MONEY MONEY ............................................................20
   *17 Why more than one session?.......................................20*
   *18 So, how many sessions do you think it will take?........20*
   *19 How much ...................................................................21*
   *20 Shouldn't we do it for free?.........................................22*
   *21 So how much should I charge?....................................23*
   *22 When do I pay? ...........................................................24*
COMMONLY ASKED CLIENT QUESTIONS .........................................26
   *23 Can I have a free session?...........................................26*
   *24 Do you accept credit card payments?..........................27*
   *25 Do you offer discounts? ..............................................27*
   *26 Do I get my money back if it doesn't work?................28*
   *27 What if I can't make the appointment on the day?....29*
   *28 Can I pay next time? ...................................................29*

*29 If it doesn't work, do I get another session for free?...30*
*30 Do I get a discount if I pay up front?............................30*
*31 Some final points to consider:.......................................30*
WHAT TO DO WHEN THINGS GO WRONG ...........................................32
HOW TO TURN ALMOST ANYONE INTO A HIGHLY SUGGESTIBLE SUBJECT 33
*32 If you can hypnotise your mother you can hypnotise anyone ...............................................................................33*
*33 Wait for the Willingness................................................39*
*34 Be interested in them and in you .................................40*
*35 Get some success happening .........................................41*
*36 Enjoy the process... and repeat!....................................42*
*37 Why hypnosis scripts are bad for you ...........................43*
COMMON CLIENT ISSUES ............................................................46
*38 Finding out what the real issue is! ...............................47*
*Three common client issues and how to fix them!............49*
*39 Phobia ...............................................................................49*
*40 Stop Smoking ..................................................................51*
*41 Weight Loss.....................................................................52*
*42 What to do when you hear, "I don't think I was hypnotised!" ......................................................................54*
*Stage one: ............................................................................56*
*Stage two:.............................................................................56*
*Stage three: .........................................................................57*
*Stage four: ...........................................................................57*
*Stage five: ............................................................................57*
*How to tell what they are really thinking..........................61*
*43 Eye Accessing Cues.........................................................61*
*Magical Eye Movements....................................................62*
*1. Make them look down .......................................................64*
*2. Make them look up .......................................................64*
*44 He's a right pain in the neck, a thorn in my side, or worse! ...................................................................................65*
*45 The biggest secret almost nobody knows to solving your biggest problem. ........................................................67*
*Advice on answering questions..........................................70*

- *46 You are rubbish / you are amazing.* ...................................73
- *Accentuating the Positive* ...................................73
- *Working with the Negative* ...............................74
- *1. Response Recognition.* ...................................75
- *2. Detach the Catch:* ..........................................76
- *3. Get curious not furious:* ................................76
- *47 The ultimate secret to happiness is…* ...........77
- *What makes you feel happy?* ...........................78
- *So what DO you want?* .....................................81
- *A happy hypnotist is a good hypnotist* ............83
- *48 How to make yourself happy in 4 easy steps* ..............83
- AND FINALLY, REMEMBER TO TURN THEM INTO A CHICKEN ...............85
- *49 Stage Hypnosis or Hypnotherapy?* ..............85
- *After the session:* ..............................................86
- *Explanations of Hypnosis* .................................87
- *50 So, how do you explain Hypnosis in just two minutes flat?* .........................................................................88
- THANK YOU FOR READING! .......................................................90

# Marketing

# How to get more clients

## 1 Take Action Now or Don't

When I have some money to spare, when I retire, when I have more experience, when I know I am perfect, when I never fail, when I am older, when I am wiser, when people tell me I am good enough, THEN I will start/expand my business – you can do nothing about what has happened already though your tomorrows are depending on YOU TODAY, YOU NOW, to make the success happen.

I began in the personal development field by hosting 'pre-retirement' courses for a large Government department and boy, did those lovely people teach me lots. So many years can go by waiting to be perfect or for whatever it is you think you need to allow yourself the chance; then retirement comes along and all some want to do is sit in the garden or sleep. I hope you age like Dick Van Dyke or similar with vigour and enthusiasm for life well into the third age, though many recognise a depletion of energy and motivation later in life. NOW is the time to take action or don't.

## 2 Beating Yourself Up

Choose to recognise what marketing efforts did NOT work as feedback, information, experience well received, 'thank you very much for whittling down what to do so I can focus on something more productive for myself' kind of attitude is helpful I find.

All experience is valuable and what works for some may not work for you, what brought Paul McKenna success may not be your own personal cup of tea. Finding your way is part of the fun, trust me, of being successful. Imagine the reaction of the interviewer when you recall the tale of your first big break, *'Really, that's what worked for you? Brilliant, well it obviously paid off!'*

## 3 If it works do it

If you are running an advertisement in the local paper for two months and had no clients from it, wonder WHY?

Really, wonder. Do not allow yourself to be fobbed off by the advertising team who tell you it will take time for you to get noticed, you want them to re-position your ad, give advice on the photograph (you DO have a photo don't you; imperative!) change the heading, whatever, though do something ELSE that works. One interview on the radio or speaking to the checkout lady at the supermarket, or threatening to hypnotise your noisy neighbour (loudly) may bring in more clients than an unnoticeable newspaper ad nestled next to weight control pills and body building powders ... I am just saying, take control of your presence in the paper if you go that way. If others are getting business that way, note how they are doing it.

## 4 Free pays off

These get you air time on local radio (as long as you tell them!) and FREE space in the newspaper (as long as you tell them!). Folks will show up just to see what's going on and see you do something to someone else and just might offer themselves up for hypnosis themselves.

The very least is you get to talk to a group of people about what you love and how brilliant hypnosis is. When people meet you face to face they are more inclined to come for therapy and recommend friends too. You can sell CDs or give out cards and leaflets, sell booklets and give dates of the next workshops to bring their friends. They can sign up RIGHT THERE AND THEN for their therapy session or buy it for their friend for their birthday.

# 5 The Clubs

Sports performance, losing weight (oh you know I hate that term but, meeting the client where they are, they are in the gym and they want to 'lose weight' so go get 'em).

Remember these places are full of people, each one potentially talking about you to someone else. One particularly unfruitful evening I felt very disheartened until it was the staff themselves who booked a few sessions for me to help them. You never know who is listening. These were the people just saw me standing there with a sign behind me and booked me up, without me saying a word! Also, you never know who visits these places, hairdressers, swimsuit models toning up for a shoot tomorrow, minor celebrities, store owners, taxi drivers, they could all be interested in hypnosis and they all talk to other people….

## 6 Focused Workshops

Weight Loss , smoking cessation, stress reduction, improve your golf, presentation anxiety (MUCH more prevalent than you would imagine) etc. Even if no one turns up, you get space in the local paper or the card is still in that corner shop you went into to buy a drink from before the talk, to tell them you were hiring the village hall to do a workshop. You DID tell them didn't you?

## 7 Back to School

Participate in a fund raiser for the school, give a hypnosis session as a prize in their raffle, do a session with a group of teachers at lunchtime to relax, Lord they need it! At a parents evening I noticed a teacher hobbling away and asked if she had a back problem (I recognised the wincing signs) and I really thought this teacher was a great teacher for my child and didn't want her to be off work!

She was absolutely NOT interested in hypnosis, though I popped a CD in the next day for her and a couple of days later she was on the 'phone telling me how much better she was because of it. Some might say that I gave away a CD for free, however I had a vested interest in keeping her in school to benefit my child, so I received payment in that way. I then received several bookings from the school, which were paid sessions.

## 8 Accelerated learning programs

What about some fun 'I bet I can make you move your finger' demo for them? ALSO, remember, photos photos photos, with the headmaster, with a large group with the school in the background – you DID bring your camera didn't you?

## 9 Your car can make you a star

Magnetic signs are cheap and fun and easy and do not hurt your Jaguar. Be brave, use the word HYPNOSIS and your phone number and just watch how many people ask you about it when you pull in for petrol, pick the kids up from school or visit the doctors. Allow yourself more time as you will have to always be polite and friendly when you may be in a rush!

# 10 Everywhere you go people ought to know

Name tags, get one. Wear it. Always. Let people tease you, so what. Get known. Go to events and get known by having a different name tag. Be different. Be you.

I used to go around with a big STOP sign on my back and folks would ask me, 'Why are you wearing a STOP sign on your back, to which I would say, 'What do YOU want to stop, everyone wants to stop something...' Get yourself known, your way.

## 11 Loud and proud

When someone asks you why you are wearing a name tag on your day off in the supermarket, talk about hypnosis and talk LOUDLY. I lost count of the number of times one person who approached me walked away as another tapped me on the shoulder, 'I couldn't help overhearing....' Checkouts are the best, talk to the staff, they love to have someone to take an interest in them or to be distracted from the hundreds of other buyers who have ignored them or have been rude. Then, everyone in the queue hears the conversation too.

## 12 Being a Groupie

No, you don't have to pretend to be an alcoholic to get into AA, just tell them you would like to speak to the group, give the facilitator a break. Speak up at your local business group meeting, you DO go to a business group meeting, don't you? Join Chamber of Commerce or Small Business Meet up in the Village Hall With A Free Biscuit who call themselves something interesting group.... Create a support group for lonely hypnotists.... Just kidding. Churches, yes, they love us, go there, speak, join all their groups, do stuff for them, on them, with them, do charitable things, enjoy.

## 13 Article Writing

Write a column in the local paper, in the church newsletter, in the parish council gazette, toilet room walls (not really!) ... though write for anyone and anything that will have you! Never, never, never, I mean, never, pay to get yourself in a publication when you are doing them a favour by writing your interesting stuff for them. Soon they will pay you to contribute regularly. Trust me.

## 14 Cashing in on Coupons

Two for one deals, bring a friend for half price, gift certificates, 50% off, it all works. Find out what works best. Do it.

## 15 Event Listings

Tell papers, publications, what's on guides, what to do in Little Hampton in the rain guides, what you are doing and where you are doing it. Online, on paper, get in there. Create a weekly event, weight group, relaxation for baton twirlers, whatever, get yourself listed.

## 16 Taking the Pressure Off

Avoid the one hit wonder. Always follow up. You are worried they can't afford a second session? Then don't do the first, your reputation is at stake and your confidence. Or do it for free, as long as you don't feel taken advantage of and you benefit in some way. Free sessions can build your confidence, promote your skills to others etc, though recognise those that don't want to pay because they don't think hypnosis works.

# Money Money Money

### 17 Why more than one session?

You do not want to be left wondering if it worked when they may be telling everyone else it didn't. If you really want to help them and they are strapped for cash, reduce your price, but get them in for that follow up session. More sessions means more income for you and more success for your clients so you both win and that's got to be a good thing.

### 18 So, how many sessions do you think it will take?

It will take as many as the presenting problem needs it to take, though I advise three to four. Realise that you are doing your client an injustice by harping on that it will be done in one session, even if you think it will and, you know, there will be more stuff coming up for them once this particular issue is fixed. You are also putting a lot of pressure on yourself to find another twenty clients a week, that's just going on four a day. Finding eighty new clients every month is a task and a half and even if you do, are ALL of them going to be totally problem free in just one session? Be caring, be real, be sensible, practical and supportive and confident by having the feedback and giving them what they need.

# 19 How much

The sad thing is, many hypnotherapists give up the profession and return to the day job because they are wanting to help people and forget they need to help themselves too. Let's bring a bit of balance here so you can do what you love AND be paid well too. When you charge a decent amount of money for services delivered, whatever that service is, you have the satisfaction that the customer is valuing the service and prepared to offer money in exchange for something valuable. Knowing this inspires you to do your very best for them and put all you can into helping them for the time and skill they are paying for. They are coming to you because this is something they cannot do for themselves, just like you go to a dentist because you can't pull out your own teeth. You don't, do you?

If you do not value the service you are providing then your client will sense that and not be confident that the change can happen for them, or that you are competent enough. They may, however, think that you are a millionaire and do this for the love of it, though this tends to be the exception! If someone has been struggling with a condition for twenty years or more and you help them free themselves from it in an hour or so, then don't you think that is a valuable service worthy of your efforts and quantifiable in monetary terms? Fair exchange for services rendered.

## 20 Shouldn't we do it for free?

Doing things for others for free is great when you don't feel miffed about being taken advantage of and truly want to do it just because you want to do it. You will start to tell which folks are really in need of that free session because you will feel so good about helping them anyway, that it is a reward in itself, or it serves to promote the fact that you actually know what you are doing and can help people. This is often, in the beginning, to friends and family who do not yet see you as a therapist and they are the hardest to prove it to! Sometimes, of course, you need to prove it to yourself that you have what it takes, or recognise where to tweak your skills to become the best you can be.

# 21 So how much should I charge?

Do your market research. It's dependent upon location, what the market expects, plus your own comfort zones and need for food. If you do not get this right, you could be back at working for others in no time. Someone somewhere will want you to work hard at something you don't like in order to make money out of you. Beware of being the cheapest, as clients expect to get what they pay for and sometimes offering cheaper prices means that folks think you won't be as good as the higher priced therapist.

Test the market. If your prices are too high or too low, you will get few clients. Experiment with positioning your price in the mid-range of other local therapists.

Ultimately your clients will let you know. The client is king.

## 22 When do I pay?

Some therapists ask for money up front and won't get out of bed until the money is in the bank. Does that sound merciless to you? I apologise. There is money to be made and tactics and strategies to use and this is where you become the professional you wish to become. There is no judgement here, really. In fact I 'said' it in that manner to see if you internally agreed with me! This is completely down to yourself.

When I started in Practice I always said to folks on the 'phone that, 'Well, you never pay until the end anyway, when you know that it has worked.' This comforted them, giving the unsaid clause that if they were not satisfied then they did not have to pay. It never happened. Everyone paid. It took all the risk out of the experience for the client, however, which I thought was important. I put myself in their position and realised that I would have been worried too, not knowing anything about the scary hypnotist or the Profession. The awkwardness, yes I did feel awkward, (strange isn't it, I never felt awkward accepting my salary from past bosses) of asking for payment at the end was entirely solved for me when I bought a tin cash box!

Accidentally, I discovered that merely by opening a drawer and rattling the tin at the end of a session, where usually everyone has forgotten about payment, was a reminder to the client that payment was now due and they would apologise and quickly search for their purse or cheque book.

I now ask for payments up front because it is easier for me and some people like to pay by credit or debit card online and not have to worry about fiddling with cash on the day of therapy. There are times when I will take cash on the day too, though this is becoming the exception. As my time becomes scarcer, so folks seem more keen to know I will be there for them so paying is a way of them ensuring that help.

# Commonly asked client questions

## 23 Can I have a free session?

When I first began I had a huge sign above the premises which said 'First Session Free' and clients queued up. I intended to give a ten minute consultation and then book them in for the proper session. What completely surprised me, however, is that quite often someone said, 'I'm sorry but I don't think I need to come back to see you, I feel so much better now!' You might think that was a bad business move, I did! However, they told lots of other people who DID come and pay me for sessions so I became known very quickly. One thing that worked well was, I would say the first 20 minutes is completely free of charge. I then let them know when the 20 minutes was up and asked if they wanted to continue. They always said yes and I would bill them at the end.

# 24 Do you accept credit card payments?

Oh, yes, and if they wanted to pay by card, back then, I would ask them to visit the local ATM round the corner and I would meet them downstairs in a short while. They always came back to pay me too!

In the modern day, taking card payments is easier with all sorts of online facilities and often clients prefer that method. Test it out, ask them.

# 25 Do you offer discounts?

Have a word with yourself and see if you want to do the usual practice of giving a discount to older folks or unemployed. Be ready with your answer. There is no right or wrong answer.

# 26 Do I get my money back if it doesn't work?

A weight control client once asked my colleague, 'what happens if it doesn't work?' to which they replied, 'well, you won't lose weight then'.

What I mean to say here is that clients often are not direct. They can be uncomfortable about the subject of money too. What they mean is will you give them the money back? What do you think? I had one client who wanted me to stop him smoking by doing some sort of mind control thing where he was not involved in the process at all. It was never going to work and yet I tried and tried and tried. It was in the early days and I got to the end of the session (two and a half hours' later) and did not want his money. He insisted on paying saying that he had used a lot of my time and was very grateful for my efforts. He said he knew I could have been seeing another client and appreciated my seeing him. I am glad he said that. I did not take his money. Though now I think he may have been right. My personal ethics did not allow me to charge for a process I was happy with. Though now with more discernment, I would not treat until resolving the motivation.

# 27 What if I can't make the appointment on the day?

Is it a genuine excuse, did some real reason prevent their attendance? As you know, often the subconscious presents obstacles to change at the last minute. Having a policy whereby the client pays 50% if they cancel within 24 hours for example prevents this. It is up to you. I know of no one that enforces this policy, but putting in on your website or card makes folks know you want them to attend, or at least to let you know they can't attend, as a courtesy to prevent you sitting and waiting....

# 28 Can I pay next time?

This is a judgement call on your part. I would say, no.

## 29 If it doesn't work, do I get another session for free?

If you have given the client your time and skill you deserve to be paid. The continued success of the treatment is the client's responsibility. A good reply to the client is "I am creating for you a window of opportunity for change. It is your responsibility to make the change."

## 30 Do I get a discount if I pay up front?

No. I work in the health profession, I am not a discount store.

## 31 Some final points to consider:

Being cheap can send out a signal that you are not the best. Someone down the road could not be offering a good service and earn more than you because of the perception of 'You get what you pay for'.

Being cheap can impact on the entire Profession. If enough Practitioners did it, the public would begin to expect a cheap therapy session and we all start to be undervalued after all the training you have invested in, in order to provide a quality service, plus your money spent on marketing and other expenses.

Being cheap can be done by others. For clients who really can't afford to pay full price, there are therapists without overheads who are working out of their front room or who visit people in need. There are therapists who really don't need to rely on money earned from their therapy sessions as they have income elsewhere. There are newly qualified therapists who welcome doing the therapy for them for free to get the experience they need. It doesn't have to be you, you can rest assured there are therapists out there to do it and clients enough for everyone.

Be good to your clients and be good to yourself. Be fair and honest and consider valuing yourself, your clients and your time. Be the best in the business.

# What to do when things go wrong

# How to turn almost anyone into a highly suggestible subject

## 32 If you can hypnotise your mother you can hypnotise anyone

Firstly, in my not so humble opinion, hypnosis is happening all day, every day as we humans continually try to get our way with just about everyone else. We often don't notice this until there is a conflict and we don't like it.

Conscious and unconscious manipulation begins from the first time we cry and get milk to the last time you questioned somebody's love for you because they don't wash up as much as you would like, or they didn't make you a coffee when they made themselves one, or didn't buy you that thing you wanted for Christmas even after all those hints!  Now this can be spouses, children, colleagues or even ourselves!  ('I vow to never buy any more chocolate as soon as Easter is over this year, because if I don't see it I won't want, it will I?')  or, ('If I put the exercise bike right in the middle of the lounge, then I am sure to use it every morning, aren't I, because I have to practically trip over the thing to get out the door!') No? Oh, just me then!

From the moment contact is established between you and the subject of your focus, you are hypnotising them, whether you realise it or not. I tell my students that, after learning these skills, you cannot stop yourself from using them.

Think about it for a moment. Whether you are aware of the choice to do so, as soon as you are introduced to an improved way of doing something, anything, you know some part of you is going to be experimenting with it. As humans we are curious creatures and, it could be said, somewhat lazy, in that we are constantly on the lookout (consciously and unconsciously) for better, easier, more effective, quicker, sleeker, sharper, ways of doing just about anything. It may be one of our greatest attributes;

certainly fuelling our constant inventiveness and responsible for the continual evolving of the labour saving device.


You may initially spend an inordinate amount of time in conversation in order to express your new eagerness to help just about anyone who will stand still long enough, though your unconscious will soon learn. One general rule of thumb is to not give out your skills without invitation and to not continue without appreciation. That appreciation can take various forms, one of which being of course, hard cash. Having a client sitting in front of you, expecting your effective help and clutching a handful of notes is truly a gift from the gods. They will leave your presence free of whatever dilemma is troubling them because they have fulfilled the criteria for being hypnotised. This also though poses the question of how do we hypnotise or even influence (is there a difference?) a loved one or friend or complete stranger that we would like to help feel better when they have no concept of hypnosis. Don't even try to explain, is the easy way. Just do this.


Timing is everything, as well as meeting your client where they are, even though they may not know themselves and of course being a brilliant hypnotherapist which reading this will help you become!

As a newly qualified hypnotherapist, your reignited mind will seek opportunities to intervene at sometimes the most inappropriate of times and localities. I liken this to a situation with my own child sitting in the back of the car when I was about to change lanes at a very tricky traffic junction when I was suddenly innocently asked, "Where were the dinosaurs when Adam and Eve got married?"

Sound familiar to any parents out there? There may have been many times past when you longed to explain your own complex belief system to your offspring and there was never a glimmer of interest … why now? It's time, that's all. The child's mind has reached a level of processing whereby further input is necessary, and then it will seek to validate the answer by evaluating it in its own terms to make it 'real'.

Often the deeper processing of your own mind will excite at the ability to clarify and even solve some tormenting challenge currently being experienced by a loved one, friend or stranger at the bus stop. The important point to mention here is the value of intention. The aforementioned child actually invited your input; different to a parent preaching their beliefs at an unwilling audience.

Now, you have changed. Whether you know the answers or not, wait for the invitation, the genuine invitation. That is, unless of course, you have too many friends already.

Trouble is, you probably won't notice the invitation when it comes. It may sound like this, 'I bet you can't hypnotise me!' Bingo. Alternatively, it may sound like this, 'Can ANYONE be hypnotised then?' Or this, 'I don't believe in any of that rubbish'.

Conversely, sometimes the most easy folks to hypnotise are the ones that resist the most as their consciousness is so tied up with resisting what you might 'do to them' that the back door is wide open to trance.

What if there is no invitation and you really want to help them? Create an opportunity for curiosity. This is all it takes. However, you have to be a little wise here and drop something into the conversation that leads to questioning.  Also, resilience is a good thing to have in such circumstance because as soon as you start dropping in anecdotes or reports on successes it is a short trip from 'I don't believe in all that hocus pocus' to 'I don't believe in YOU'.

There is a myriad of ways to entice and entrance new subjects to seek out your talents and become your paying client, there are however a few rules.  Those who have read my other books know the value of being WISE.

WISE is my acronym for the following qualities.

1 Being **Willing**

2 Being **Interested**

3 Having **Success**

4 **Enjoy**ing that Success.

# 33 Wait for the Willingness

Don't do what I did and tell everyone in your enthusiastic exuberance that you can hypnotise people to be happier and healthier and you want to change the world as you are so excited - someone will knock it out of you!


When you wait for however you are communicating with to be WILLING, truly willing, then the rest is easy. Curiosity mounts as soon as anyone knows you are a hypnotist and part of the challenge of the newly qualified hypnotherapist is to stay strong and resolute as loving(!) friends and family tease one relentlessly with comments such as, 'Go on then, hypnotise me now!'  This is a form of willingness, yes, though welcomed for those of ten years' standing and met with a sly internal grin, this challenge is to be avoided at all costs when your experience and ego is on the low side!  The best approach I would advise with the teasing elder brother or unbelieving spouse is to let that opportunity pass you right by and wait until they are relaxed, watching TV or engrossed in some passionate hobby and then get all Ericksonian with them, using metaphor and shared memories of specific incidents to get agreement and rapport on a deeper level.

## 34 Be interested in them and in you

What's the point otherwise? We are going beyond logic and reason now; no more 'because I need lots of clients and have bills to pay' and the like, let's pretend that stuff is not an issue right now. We can get to all that later. To trance or not to trance: you need experience and let them pay you when they are sitting in your therapy room convinced you can help them, or desperate enough that they have tried everything else and all that has failed.

When you are truly and obviously interested in another human being, rather than just waiting your turn to get your own point across, something magical happens. This is the root of why so many folks have affairs and indiscretions, because feelings of being out on one's own, feeling lonely and misunderstood and ignored within the mundane day to day living are rampant. Whilst this process may be taken advantage of by those seeking temporary gratification of the flesh(!) there is something so very special in really taking an interest in another and going beyond one's judgments of them and their condition.

In fact, the reasons why some trances fail have more to do with the therapist's blockages than the clients.  Your own 'baggage' can be triggered by a client, or stranger on a bus even, fellow patron at a restaurant, etc, just looking similar to someone you knew years' ago.  A shadow of the same expression that cut you to the core when you were eight years old suddenly appears on their face!  A certain accent, tone of voice, profession, sexual orientation, it's like we are sometimes just waiting to be offended!

So, when I say be interested, I mean go beyond yourself and be curious about them and their situation.  Also, very importantly, be interested in what you may be able to say back to help or hinder.  Usually, we are better at the latter!

## 35 Get some success happening

Talk for a while and change your body position, scratch your nose, your cheek, touch your toes! DO something and make yourself influential.  The world is different merely because you are here so test it out and after you have nodded and made the right noises for a while in gaining rapport with someone, shuffle your feet, look down, turn around, perhaps look at your watch and wait for them to say, 'sorry, do you need to go?' Or 'what's the time?' Be influential, get some success happening that let's you know they are listening from an UNCONSCIOUS perspective.  Take a nice, deep breath and sit back and notice them do the same; if they don't keep weaving things in until you catch them almost copying you and following your lead.  If this doesn't happen, walk away, you'd be bored out of your mind anyway and they aren't interested in you at all!

Or, SAY something.  Say something like, 'I really have to face up to things right now' Or, 'on the face of it, it all seems ok' Or, 'I get so irritated when I don't face up to things'. Or, 'we are only scratching the surface here', or 'who NOSE what might happen if...'.  See if your partner scratches their face and hey presto.

# 36 Enjoy the process… and repeat!

Now you have that success flowing, do not jump up and down and tell them how brilliant you are (I know it is tempting), just use that success to give you a little lift and the inspiration to do another influential thing, pace and lead until you lead them into trance.

# 37 Why hypnosis scripts are bad for you

So there you are, with your 'Blushing' and 'Confidence' scripts stacked neatly on the desk with various scribbles to personalise the experience for Hilary, the high-flying trainee lawyer, who wants confidence to stop her blushing inappropriately.

It will soon cease to amaze you that your client could quite typically, within minutes, go from, "I don't know why I'm here really, I'm a very sceptical person and you are not going to make me cluck like a chicken or anything are you?" (again with the clucking, I often feel like adding it into the trance just to validate the preconception), to "Can you do something for my asthma whilst you're there, and get rid of the wart on my knee, as I've heard you people can do that".

After diplomatically condensing all you would like to deliver in response into an acceptable management of expectations for the eager Hilary, you confidently begin the trance induction, confirming what it is she has told you she wants help with. "So you are here because you have been experiencing inappropriate blushing and ..." Interrupting, as she is just closing her eyes (and reminding you how the unconscious will always put you right), she murmurs, "Yes, but I drink heavily to conceal the fact."

Casting aside the assembled scripts and thoughtful aide memoirs, you immediately grapple quietly through the various stacks of paperwork under the desk to secure the 'Alcohol' script as she eases into a blissfully tranquil state whilst you actually feel your lower lumbar disc pop out.

Whilst it is useful, initially, to thoroughly digest just about anything worthy of your examination in the appropriate realm of 'Blushing' or however else the client initially diagnoses their dilemma, it will serve you well to commit such material to memory with perhaps key phrases to jog them out of your own unconscious hoards when necessary. Then you will competently apply the appropriate key elements of the required therapeutic interventions with little risk to your own wellbeing and skeletal structure.

# Common Client Issues

# 38 Finding out what the real issue is!

You quickly learn that often the conscious mind has little true idea of the nature of the problem, though, my goodness it tries its best to guess.

That leaves us with a dilemma: if the client isn't telling themselves the truth, how do you think they are going to tell you? The solutions of course are within the unconscious mind and our duty is to create an environment and an opportunity for (a) the client to reveal the intricacies of the problem to themselves and (b) for us to make it safe enough for them to tell us about it. Now this is as true for the professional hypnotist as it is for you really really really wanting to help your best friend who does not believe in any of this mumbo jumbo but loves you dearly!

I have often said, 'thank goodness people smoke', because they would probably never consider hypnosis in any other circumstance other than to stop smoking and also because such sessions are of such important learning value to the new hypnotherapist. It soon becomes clear that they are really ready to stop smoking when you experience what I have often called 'the Obi One Kenobi moment'. That is, that after the patches, the chewing gum, the 'let's all get together in a small room and talk about the perils of smoking' groups have not worked, together with other more bizarre treatments, they announce you are the last hope on the list, 'I've tried everything else and nothing works'.

Either they want to strike the last known hope from the list and announce to the spouse, 'That's it, there is absolutely no hope left now so stop nagging me', or you sense that somehow they will make this final procedure work for them because actually they do sincerely want to stop.

The following section revisits what we already know of hypnosis whilst delivering certain key points to the client. Always remember whatever views you held about the subject before your teachings and realise your client is often vulnerable, perhaps somewhat desperate and despite that, still wary or even cynical of the approach.

# Three common client issues and how to fix them!

## 39 Phobia

Step one is to establish what is causing the phobic reaction. In this example we will use spiders. You have been professionally trained, I know; though this is a simple, condensed refresher so, bear with.

Ask the client what is it about spiders that causes the phobic reaction. Often the client will say that it is when they see a spider running. Ah, movement then. We are usually okay if the stressor stays put and does not bother us. So thinking it will leap from some unseen place and purposively target the client with malice aforethought, had it the capacity for such complexity of thought, is interesting.

The next step is to ask them to briefly describe the worst phobic response they have ever had to spiders. When they reach the end of the story ask then to tell you on a scale of one to ten just how anxious they are right now with zero being totally relaxed and ten being totally anxious. Often the client will give a number of seven or higher.

Now distract the client from the spider anxiety by asking them about their trip to your clinic or would they like a glass of water etc. Yes, a break state moment provides necessary relief and enables recalibration.

The next step is to put the client into a light trance and ask them to imagine that there is a control room in their mind. In this control room they will discover a dial that controls the reaction to their phobia. Let's say that in the pre talk they said their anxiety was at a seven. You now ask them to see the dial at number seven and they are now reaching out and turning it down to a one or a two.

The next step is to bring them out of trance and ask them to have a think about spiders and ask them how much lower on the scale they are now in terms of their reaction to them. The majority of clients will report a much lower rating on the scale.

Congratulate the client on a job well done.

## 40 Stop Smoking

The first step is to ask the client what do they find tastes or smells totally disgusting. For example a food they hate or perhaps dog excrement or vomit etc.

The second step is to put your client into a trance. Now ask them to imagine themselves in a small room filled with their disgusting thing. Now they notice that their cigarettes are mixed into the disgusting thing. They have to reach into the disgusting thing to pull out a cigarette. Once they have pulled out a cigarette say to the client that their cigarette is covered in the disgusting thing. Now and forever more every time they try to put a cigarette into their mouth they can taste and smell the disgusting thing. Be sure to anchor this physically with your client.

The next step is to bring them out of trance and ask them to try and put one of their disgusting flavoured cigarettes in their mouth. The majority of clients won't be able to or will actually refuse to even try. Congratulate the client on a job well done.

# 41 Weight Loss

The first step is to ask the client what food is holding them back from their weight loss success. Most clients say biscuits or fast food or large portion sizes. In this case let's say the client says fast food.

The second step is to put your client into a trance. Now say to the client that their subconscious mind will now do all of the work for them in order to achieve their weight loss success. They don't even need to listen to what you are about to say next. They can just sit back, relax and enjoy floating away in a relaxing state of trance while their subconscious does all of the work for them.

The next step is to say "I would now like your subconscious mind to come up with three new behaviours that will replace eating that old fast food. Whatever it was that fast food used to do for you your subconscious will now create three new positive behaviours that are even more fulfilling than that old fast food used to be. Your subconscious mind may not show you what these new behaviours are right now but when the time is right they will just happen automatically and naturally. While you just sit back and relax I will now give your subconscious mind twenty seconds to create and install these new positive behaviours". Slowly count from twenty down to zero.

The next step is to bring the client out of trance and explain to them that the new behaviours will just happen automatically and naturally over the next few days.

Congratulate the client on a job well done.

# 42 What to do when you hear, "I don't think I was hypnotised!"

What is hypnosis? I ask the question almost daily of my eager students even when the answer is supposedly apparent.

"A relaxed focused state of concentration", they offer, correctly, as I then go on to explain that this is just what I told them yesterday. Today we may have a new definition.

"It's the bypass of the critical factor", offers another, again correctly, referring to something else I may have said at some point.

When folks pay good money and hang on your every word, there's a duty to ensure that the word is true. With hypnosis and its varying theories as to why it works, there are an awful lot of words to evaluate and these often change according to who you are speaking to. Though, let me be clear, the two definitions thus offered are indeed correct.

Modern models or theories of hypnosis generally fall into two camps that is state related or non state. Hilgard, who we shall focus on again later, is a classic state theory model. Simply put, he proposed that there is a hidden part of us, termed a hidden observer, which dwells within us and is part of us, though distinctly separate. Hilgard's theory requires the subject to be in a certain state before hypnosis can take place.

Non state models offer the idea that we don't need to be put into any sort of special state of mind and/or body because we naturally fluctuate and drift in and out of varying states of conscious and unconscious processing on a continual basis, it is kind of natural and easy to do this and the hypnotist is merely engaging with a natural and normal functioning of the subject when doing their hypnotising of the subject.

Hassett & White (1989) stated that hypnosis be defined as a state of awareness induced by specific techniques and affecting changes in thought, perception, and behaviour.

Definitions and explanations of hypnosis are still the subject of much discussion and dispute. In my experience, the general public's (of which we are all part of by the way) contemplation of hypnosis goes something like this. Forgive me using smoking as an example; it could be losing weight or stopping eating biscuits as the subject is dangerously diabetic etc. It begins.

## Stage one:

Hypnosis? Don't be so silly there's no such thing is there?

## Stage two:

Oh, I get it now, that is when some guy makes people do things against their will, like cluck like a chicken on stage to make the audience laugh, well that will never happen to me thank you very much.

## Stage three:

Right, so I've tried everything I can to stop smoking and the doctor says I will actually die shortly if I continue to do this and I cannot stop by myself. Maybe if a hypnotist can make someone do daft things on stage against their will, I can go to a hypnotist to get them to stop me smoking.

## Stage four:

What are they going to do to me? How does it work?

## Stage five:

Turns out I still have no idea how it works but it did and I don't want a cigarette. Weird.

My point is here, that even though I am now going into the definitions and theories of hypnosis, to the subject who really wants it to work, for whatever reason, it will work. Still, it may not matter to the subject being hypnotised, though it matters to those teaching it and defending the profession, so we continue. Maybe we can be content to use the analogy that we suddenly unconsciously yank our hand away from something [a hot stove, a sharp knife, a tickly spider] and then consciously set about figuring out why. Hypnosis is the same, it works, then we try and figure out why.

One of my favourite models is The Generalised Reality-Orientation concept which when first proposed by Shor in 1959 puts forth that humans have a 'background against which to measure events and implement operative-decision-making.

Reality, our own personal version of it, is continually being updated by new information and experiences and so is constantly in a process of adaptation. Shor proposed that "any state in which the GRO has faded to relative non-functional unawareness may be termed a trance state" so, again this is a state theory. Being so faded into the background, critical factors that seemed originally immutable seem to be completely disregarded and therefore the hypnotist's suggestion is given air time, so to speak.

What we hypnotists rely upon is this. When you have experienced something and realise it gives you a better life experience, you will continue to do it. That sounds easy doesn't it? This is how I reason all these models and theories out. Do something different (having bypassed the critical factor which would have thrown it out) and find that life is better, the unconscious will continue to do it, naturally, easily and without question. Take microwaves; look how dubious the world was generally and the housewife was particularly when microwaves came into the kitchen. I myself remember my mom and I looking at it sitting there freshly out of the box in the middle of the living room, wondering, how on earth can this thing cook something in seconds that it takes hours to cook in a conventional oven? Though, today, I would readily accept microwaving my Christmas pudding for three minutes rather than boiling on the hob for an hour and a half.

Imagine the critical factor as being the gatekeeper standing on the threshold between conscious and unconscious thought.

Find an easier way and you will keep doing it, if it gives you what IT thinks is a better life (based on what it has been programmed to believe). That is the duty of your unconscious mind after all, to give you a better life experience.

So, what is hypnosis? When your state dependent, hidden observer, hiding behind its critical factor in your general reality orientation finally figures it out, please let me know.

# How to tell what they are really thinking

## 43 Eye Accessing Cues

It is difficult to think effectively without some unconscious movement of the eyes.

Notice how a child needs to look around whilst formulating a response to your questioning. As you demand a young child looks at you whilst they are answering they are then unable to answer.

You cannot think without feeling

You cannot feel without thinking

However,

You can think and deny the feelings

You can feel and deny the thoughts

That intricate connection of thoughts and feelings is called emotion. As the

central processing unit for all our emotions, memories, external stimuli and internal

responses, the brain is a complex organ to say the least. To understand how an

individual processes internal information and to predict how they will act upon it, we

need to first understand a little about the brain and how the eye movements relate to

accessing different parts of the brain.

## Magical Eye Movements

Unconsciously, we pick up on signals being given by those communicating with us. We determine whether we think they are nervous, over-confident, willing to talk about something, or whether they wished we would go away.

We have unconsciously calibrated those we are closest to so that we know how to make them happy – and how to annoy them too!

By studiously observing an individual's eye patterns, we can get clues as to where they store related information to a specific question.

When processing information, internally, we do it either visually, auditorily, kinaesthetically, olfactorily, or gustatorily. We can access the meaning of anything in any one or any combination of the five sensory channels.

The developers of neuro linguistic programming, Bandler and Grinder, observed that people move their eyes in systematic directions, depending upon the kind of thinking they are doing at the time. They termed these clues, "eye accessing cues".

Try this exercise with your loved one, or not so loved one!

## 1. Make them look down

Talk about something, anything, that happens to be important to them. As them how they feel about it. When they are truly accessing their feelings, they will look down.

## 2. Make them look up

As them about an article of clothing, or their car, or what they think the colour of your shirt is and would it perhaps be better in blue? When they are visualising, they will look up.

Note: if you cannot by hook or crook get your loved one to look up then they may be a bit depressed!

# 44 He's a right pain in the neck, a thorn in my side, or worse!

It's also worth noting that 'People are not their behaviours' which is another Hypnosis/NLP part of our diploma training.

People do the best they can with what they have at the time, being who they are and knowing what they know at the time. The way we react to something today, is different to the way we reacted to something many years ago (Married? Me? Don't' be daft, I'll never get married….!) People have behaviours and these are manifested to us.

When you are unhappy or angry with someone (particularly a child) realise that it is the behaviour you are unhappy with, not the person. Children very quickly label themselves as a 'naughty' child and then go about learning what naughty means and demonstrate that behaviour, because, apparently, they are justified to be so!

Likewise, we can label ourselves. Defining yourself to others as being 'lazy' or 'not very confident' is not helpful. We all have the same resources available to us and can choose to learn a new behaviour. If one person can do it, anyone can LEARN to do it. We have all experienced being confident at some time in our life, and can remember and demonstrate being confident again, merely by choosing to do so.

Therefore if one person, who used to be morbidly obese, is now slim, you can do it too! If one person who used to smoke 40 cigarettes a day stopped doing so, so can you! If Arnold Swarzenegger used to be a 6 stone weakling and turned that around to become a champion body builder then....! Okay, though if we all put some time in to improve our physical fitness and ate more healthily we would certainly see a great improvement in our physical state wouldn't we?

# 45 The biggest secret almost nobody knows to solving your biggest problem.

**'You Have A Contractual Obligation to Your Self and You Don't Even Know It!**' - Let's presume you have a problem with losing weight. Substitute anything you like for the focus of your problem, the structure to solving it remains the same.

Okay. You said you want to 'lose weight'. What really happens when you say this, when you decide that this is what you want? Why do you feel so horrid and disappointed 'with yourself' if and when it doesn't work and you eat 'something you shouldn't' or you don't lose the weight? It is because you let yourself down. You welched on the deal and you fell out with you. Realise that this is what happens so many times with every diet you put yourself through. When you decide on a change of lifestyle you enter into a contract with your Self. This is the self that needs your help. Now, I know you may want to just scoot through these questions and ideas and keep on reading. Though, do yourself a favour, really, this is a favour to yourself, and write your answers down somewhere. Even better, get a friend to ask you and have a discussion. Ready?

Think of yourself as your own particular client. This client has a problem with weight control/overeating/holding onto excess energy/slow metabolism. Who knows what the real problem is? Ask your client self these questions and answer honestly. It would be fun to do this with a trusted friend (honestly, it would). When I have asked these questions of my lovely lady clients who have tried every diet on the planet before they come to me for hypnotherapy, we have often ended up in fits of laughter, which was never my plan but often unexpectedly lightened things enormously. Here goes. The preliminary questions to ask yourself are:

1. "How long have you had this problem?"

2. "When does/doesn't this problem occur?"

3. "What would we see if we were to observe this problem?"

4. "What would we see that was different if this problem were gone?"

5. "How does the client (that's you!) perceive the problem?"

6. "What stops you from resolving this problem?"

7. "What previous solutions have been attempted and how well did they work long term?"

8. "What would you lose if a solution was found?"

9. "So how would we know the solution has been found?"

10. "What function/secondary gains does this problem have"

# Advice on answering questions

Make sure you decide on the outcomes: beyond what may seem obvious, what exactly is it you want?

Make sure you have clearly defined objectives: make these objectives honest and accessible and positive.

So, stated in the positive: (remember we are not losing weight here, we are gaining health, or however positively you put it), stated in sensory-based language: get emotional about all this! For example, if it upsets you that you are not showing the world the real you, the fact that this is a problem for you tells you that it distresses you that you are not walking around in the body you would like to be in.

Make sure it is within the control of the client, (you!): ensure you are not reliant on someone else, or some potion or pill to do it for you.

Make sure it is ecological in the client's environment: are you able to put things in place in order for this to happen, e.g. take Tupperware to work?

Make sure there are measurable results: NOW I suggest you only begin measuring the results as you feel them happen. You would be surprised how many of my ladies feel slimmer, better, healthier and happier and then they get on the scales and their world comes crashing down because they have put on a pound or not lost the half stone they were sure must have come off! This is about managing expectations, go on the scales once a MONTH, though if I had my way you would chuck them out.

Measure yourself instead as you feel your clothes loosen. Keep yourself happy and positive. Do not allow any external device to tell you that you are not doing as well as you feel. Feeling is everything. Feel good first. One day you will be less able than you are now. One day you will look back at photographs of this lovely body that you disapprove of at the moment and wish you could turn back the years. Feel good for no reason, or feel good simply because you have eyes to see and ears to hear. You have a body to feel the world around you with, use it and take care of it, own it, nourish and protect it.

You have made a big fat hairy hypnotic deals with yourself so don't let yourself down, ok?

## 46 You are rubbish / you are amazing.

"Wow, aren't you good/fast/brilliant at typing/painting/writing/drawing/make up/washing up/ironing, I wish I could do that!"

## Accentuating the Positive

It is somewhat difficult to give others praise, either because it has not been usual to do so, or because regardless of what you say and how you say it the other person is filtering, deleting and distorting what you say ("they don't mean it, they want something from me...they want me to ALWAYS do the ironing....that isn't true because I'm fat and I know I look terrible …… I don't care if you think I'm good at my job, I would rather be somewhere else today…."). It also follows that just because we are good at something, it doesn't mean we have to do it for the rest of our lives! Recognising our abilities, though, is important.

Moreover, perhaps it is vital to do so. It is through recognising our accomplishments, and the gratitude of others, that we attract more of the same. Eventually, our compliments do get the message across when trust is established and the rewards to both parties are well worth pursuing.

## Working with the Negative

A comment only upsets us if, on some level of our being, we think it might be true. Think about that for a moment. If a slim girl cries when a boy calls her 'a fat cow', what does that demonstrate to us? Either she thinks she IS fat, regardless of her mother's/boyfriend's/best friend's/weight club's perception, or she HAS BEEN fat and has not come to terms with being lean, strong and healthy, or she is worried she will become fat in her future. Either way, the insult of 'fat' is an issue for her. It wouldn't have impact if the boy said her ability to store unused energy was quite remarkable and because of that he likened her to one of the most inoffensive, useful and popular animals we have on the planet! If we do not accept the idea as being true for us, it does not hurt. We may even smile.

As humans we seem very adept at filtering out those compliments and that's because we have developed a resilience to being hurt. So much is aimed at us nowadays to encourage us to part with our hard earned cash that we often think there is a 'catch' to a compliment.

However, the insults that fire us up with indignation or tears point to where the healing still needs to take place. In essence, when we are hurt or insulted we are experiencing SHAME and feel blame. We either blame ourselves for not being perfect (and who is, come on??) or blame another for bringing some (ultimately useful) hurt to our attention as it cries out to be healed. Here are some tips to 'Reframe the Shame'.

# 1. Response Recognition.

However this has come into your awareness, via best friend, worst enemy, television, magazine or billboard, recognise that it is YOUR response that has enlivened it within you. Others may have been targeted, though they just allow the information to just pass them by.

## 2. Detach the Catch:

You've been caught. Just like a fish on a hook, you have responded internally and this is useful as it reminds you of a past incident or triggered a chink in your emotional armour that can be repaired and polished. This is now nothing to do with the instigator so detach from it/them.

## 3. Get curious not furious:

The more you can be interested in your own response and wonder where it came from internally in your own experience and chose to reframe and release the past incidences, the more you release the power the instigator has over your emotional state. When you can hear the same thing in the future and smile, you're done. As long as it still smarts, go back to stage one!

# 47 The ultimate secret to happiness is…

We may be quite aware of who pushes our buttons to create a negative state within ourselves, but what pushes your Happiness Control Button — is it a chocolate bar?

What makes you happy? Let's put it another way, does the weather make you miserable? Does a spell of light drizzle mean it's a miserable day? Don't blame yourself! I still hear weathermen talk of it being a miserable day tomorrow when I watch the forecasts. So, misery loves company, remember? Though also remember that happiness is infectious.

There is no doubt that we are constantly in a state of flux. We are constantly changing state from one state to another. As good as we feel now, we may feel sad later. As sad as we feel right now we may feel very happy later. If your feelings change, like the weather, alternating apparently out of your control, then it's time to get happy. In happiness all things are possible; as this genuine positive state is so very important it deserves a little attention. Identify it. Then apply it when you really need it.

As if you have a happiness control button. What has to happen for you to feel happy right now? I hope you know. If you don't know the steps to take to cheer yourself then you may be totally reliant on another to bring you happiness, or just waiting to see if factors in your environment bring about this change of state – like the weather.

There is no doubt that life is here to challenge us, cajole us to stretch and reach and expand all that we are and all that we want to be. Pressures at home and work can bring us down, so we have to have a strategy to go higher. This is especially true if it is only certain foods or cigarettes or only red, red, wine makes you happy.

## What makes you feel happy?

What could you feel happy about, rich about, etc, how could you feel the most loved? You may wonder what all this has to do with losing weight. By the way, don't do that. Don't use the word 'lose' when you are trying to enlist the help of the most powerful part of your mind, the unconscious part, as it doesn't empower you to think in terms of loss. It is never good: whether it is losing your mind, losing a loved one, losing your way, even losing your keys is just not empowering. Your most powerful mind responds better when you seek to gain something. Gain health, vitality, be lean strong and healthy and now you are in a better frame of mind to seek that which you want. We often talk in terms of what we don't want rather than that which we do, which you will find out with NLP ideas on moving away from something negative rather than towards the positive. Okay you want to move away from being fat, though attach that idea to moving towards being lean, strong and healthy and now you have some place to go to, rather than just running away.

The unconscious mind does not recognise a negative idea. What I mean by this is that if you were told not to think of a thing you would think of it first and then try and discount it.

Don't think of telling all your friends about how great this book is.

Is it that you ALWAYS get more of what you focus upon, or that things seem worse if we constantly look at our reality and say it's not what we want, thereby seemingly creating more of it. Stop thinking about fat, fat, fat and not wanting it. Start thinking of being lean, strong and healthy instead and work with what comes up for you.

Your spiritual friends will explain that every time we pay attention to something we energise its presence within us, so (just in case they are right) it pays to strengthen positive not negative, knowing that it is all too easy to agree with someone else's hardship than acknowledge our own success. If your best friend in the whole world was bemoaning the fact that life was tough and she/he had been trying to lose weight their entire life and they always ended up fatter than before no matter how hard they try, then your slim alter ego may not readily turn round and say how easy it really is if you just put your mind to it.

# So what DO you want?

Imagine you could have it right now. Be it, have it, do it.

Right now, A miracle has happened and you CANNOT fail. Work with the essence of it and find out where you have the qualities of it right now before you hit the button. Oh, by the way, your 'button' (or 'anchor' in hypnosis/nlp terms) can be turning that ring around on your finger three times, squeezing your hands together in a very particular way, saying a certain word out loud (yes, out loud) to yourself three times, you pick! To be effective it has to be something deliberate, for what you are doing here is getting yourself to experience the qualities of happiness and then creating a kind of 'knot in the handerchief' to remind your unconscious how to do it when you really need it.

Okay. Go and feel happy. Having trouble? Well, then next time you really do feel happy THEN program your button and when you have stacked up enough occasions then you will find that when you 'press' that button during a period when you really need it, then presto, you will feel happier.

So, if you cannot think of time when you will be truly experiencing happiness within the next day or two, you know where the work is to be done. Hey, do not judge yourself; if the chocolate bar creates a sensation of happiness within you, use it for your button and then fire it off without the chocolate bar later. Who knows, it may then be that you can be happier about a much wider range of stuff!

# A happy hypnotist is a good hypnotist

# 48 How to make yourself happy in 4 easy steps

1. Create a situation/catch yourself being happy. You MUST be feeling that lift, that genuine smile on your face, that tingle of excitement or appreciation of something that catches you by surprise, feel it, feel it, feel it. Make it your mission to get happy.

2. Pinch the third knuckle on your right hand (or whatever!) at the PEAK of your happy experience.

3. Stack 'em up. Do this again and again, ONLY at times of peak happiness.

4. When you have about five or six genuine experiences stacked up, 'press your button' and sense the difference in how you feel. Brilliant!

# And Finally, Remember to Turn Them into a Chicken

## 49 Stage Hypnosis or Hypnotherapy?

When I initially set up in practice, I was very keen to promote the difference between therapeutic hypnosis and stage hypnotism. I would spend time explaining the difference and ensure that the subject knew something of what to expect, allaying fears of 'mind control' and memory recall. Knowing far more now, and having conducted many 'stage hypnosis phenomena' the divide between the two is much less defined.

Now, I work with whatever is presented to me. Such as, before the session:

"I'm worried you will take control over my mind" Gosh, I'm worried too, says I!

What a responsibility that would be. Though if I was to take control over your mind, what positive change would you want to happen?

"You're not going to make me cluck like a chicken or anything are you?"

You know, shall we just get the clucking over with because being as that is your main definition of what being hypnotised involves then you may be somewhat disappointed if it doesn't happen for you."

## After the session:

"I felt very relaxed but I'm not sure I was hypnotised" It's because we didn't do the clucking thing wasn't it? As you said you had never been hypnotised before by what criteria do you know that to be true?

# Explanations of Hypnosis

Conformist View: After two centuries of controversy hypnosis is still the subject of debate. Social theories of hypnosis, such as those propounded by Orne & Evans (1965) and Barber (1969 & et al 1974) contend that the 'hypnotised' subject is attempting to conform to the social role defined by the situation and the demands of the hypnotist. This statement needs to be weighed up with the known fact that a subject can be hypnotised into a state of somnambulism and surgically operated upon without anaesthetic. The person would have to be a very willing 'people pleaser' to conform in such a way.

# 50 So, how do you explain Hypnosis in just two minutes flat?

Summarising the above, hypnosis can be described as a discreet state of dissociated awareness of one's ordinary reality.

This state is produced by a process by which the attention is focused on a particular set of events (internal or external) leading to a relative 'fading' of generalised reality from awareness. One can then realise how common this state of mind is when applying such an explanation: when watching a good movie, listening to a boring or, indeed, engaging speaker; drifting away on a warm beach listening to the waves lapping at the shore. All of these situations include a fading of one's usual reality orientation with the focus being elsewhere.

It is in this state, freed albeit momentarily, from the rigours of living a busy life, when the mind then becomes able to substitute an alternative reality-orientation that can be used therapeutically to explore creative possibilities. Any useful changes in the derived concepts and functions can then be reintegrated into the thoughts, feelings, perceptions and thereafter, behaviour of the individual.

Sleep, jogging, half an hour in the Jacuzzi, finishing the book on the bedside table, using the hair straighteners in peace, frantic dusting, all give temporary relief from the general busyness of life when our own inner therapist makes its attempts to address our concerns. Only when that communication is blocked in some way do we need third party intervention to assist.

Oh, you really, really, really want to stop drinking/taking drugs/smoking/doing frantic dusting but you can't? Sounds like that communication might be blocked, best check out your local hypnotist and get clucking....!

# Thank you for reading!

Amazon reviews are really important to future writing projects for independent authors. Please leave a review for me because I would love to hear your thoughts about this book.

If you would like to receive your **FREE** preview of my next book please **email** info@hiprocom.com.

Thank you!

Printed in Great Britain
by Amazon